What We Believe (Third Edition)
Session Guide, Part Two (Sessions 13-24)

We welcome your comments. Call us at 1-800-333-8300 or email us at editors@faithaliveresources.org.

ISBN 978-1-59255-758-5

10 9 8 7 6 5 4 3 2

JESUS CHRIST (1)

BIBLE TRIVIA

1.   5.

2.   6.

3.   7.

4.   8.

VIDEO DISCUSSION GUIDE

1. What does the word *incarnation* mean as it applies to Jesus (see John 1:1, 14)? Why is the incarnation so important to Christians?

2. Read Genesis 1:1-2 and Matthew 1:20. How is the work of the Spirit at creation similar to the work of the Spirit in the incarnation? Why is believing in the virgin birth of Jesus important?

3. Tell what the following names mean:

- Jesus (see Matthew 1:21):

- Immanuel (see Matthew 1:23):

- Christ (see John 20:31):

4. In what general way is Jesus "the bread of life"? Also, recall the specific symbolism that Pastor Lew sees in the water, flour, sugar, oil, salt, and yeast that go into a loaf of bread.

5. What does Pastor Lew mean when he says, "Jesus is the way we see God"? See also John 14:6-7. What qualities of Jesus help you understand—and draw closer to—God the Father?

6. Reflect for a minute or two on who Jesus is to you (reading Philippians 2:5-11 may be helpful). Then complete this statement: "Jesus, to me you are . . ."

JESUS CHRIST (2)

REVIEW QUIZ

(true|false)

T | F

☐ | ☐   1. The author of the Belgic Confession is Pastor Lew Vander Meer.

☐ | ☐   1. The word *incarnation* refers to the way God came in the flesh to live in the world.

☐ | ☐   2. Though Jesus is both God and man, his deity far outweighs his humanity.

☐ | ☐   3. We believe that Jesus was conceived in the normal way, but later the Spirit filled him and he became divine as well as human.

☐ | ☐   4. The name Jesus means "eternal God."

☐ | ☐   5. The name Immanuel means "God with us."

☐ | ☐   6. Christ is Jesus' last name and means the same thing as Jesus.

☐ | ☐   7. The Old Testament name for Christ is Messiah.

☐ | ☐   8. "The Word became flesh and made his dwelling among us" comes from the book of John.

☐ | ☐   9. Jesus once said that when we look at him, we should see God.

☐ | ☐ 10. "Bread of life" is a title that applies to Jesus.

BIBLE TRIVIA

1.   5.

2.   6.

3.   7.

4.   8.

VIDEO DISCUSSION

1. How many natures and how many persons does Jesus have? Was Jesus divine part of the time, human at others? Why was it necessary for him to be both fully God and fully human?

2. As God-man, Christ was both "humiliated" and "exalted." Use the Apostles' Creed to list the five steps of Christ's humiliation and the four steps of his exaltation.

3. Suppose your chemistry grades are slipping. Instead of your usual "B"s, you're getting "C"s and "D"s. You just don't try anymore. One day after class, your teacher asks what's wrong and offers to help you. With a great deal of effort, you pull your grades back up. Your teacher is happy and says that you've atoned for your earlier lack of effort. What does the teacher mean by "atoned"? What does Christ atone for? How? And what do we mean when we say his atonement is "vicarious"?

4. What did Jesus do that Adam and Eve couldn't do? What do we mean when we say his perfection is "imputed" to us?

5. Pastor Lew says, "Jesus suffered for you. Jesus died for you. Jesus went through hell for you." Think about that, then write a short response that expresses your personal reaction to God's incredible way of paying for your sins. If you wish, write your response in the form of a note to God ("Dear God . . .").

THE CHURCH (1)

REVIEW QUIZ

T | F

☐ | ☐   1.   To atone for something means to make amends for it, to set it right.

☐ | ☐   2.   Christ atoned for our sins when he ascended into heaven.

☐ | ☐   3.   We help atone for our own sins by loving God and serving others.

☐ | ☐   4.   Part of Christ's atonement was that he had to obey God perfectly.

☐ | ☐   5.   The "at-one-ment" of Christ's atonement means that Christ brings us together with our neighbors once again.

☐ | ☐   6.   When we say Christ's atonement is vicarious, we mean he suffered and died in our place.

☐ | ☐   7.   Christ has a human and divine nature in one person.

☐ | ☐   8.   Like cream in coffee, the two natures of Christ are indistinguishable.

☐ | ☐   9.   Only Christ's divine nature is needed to save us from our sins.

☐ | ☐   10.   "The Word became flesh" describes Christ's incarnation.

BIBLE TRIVIA

1.   5.

2.   6.

3.   7.

4.   8.

VIDEO DISCUSSION GUIDE

1. What is the church? For a picture of the first church formed after Jesus ascended into heaven, read Acts 2:42-47. What went on there that still goes on in your congregation?

2. List the marks that Pastor Lew says describe what people do to make sure their church is a true church. What questions do you have about these marks?

3. Besides simply not having the marks mentioned above, how else would you describe what could be called a "false church" or a sect or a cult?

4. Do you think it's OK to date people who say they believe in God (or at least in some "divine power" that rules the world) but never go to church?

5. What three "attributes" of the true church does Pastor Lew mention? Can you think of other characteristics that you personally would look for when trying to decide on a new church home?

6. What are some of the ways God has really blessed your church?

THE CHURCH (2)

REVIEW QUIZ

(multiple choice)

_____ 1. When we say we belong to a holy catholic church, we mean that the church is (a) part of the Roman Catholic Church; (b) universal or worldwide; (c) traditional; (d) the true, biblical church.

_____ 2. Which of the following is not one of the marks of the true church that Pastor Lew discussed: (a) pure teaching/ preaching of the Word; (b) correct use of sacraments; (c) friendliness of the people; (d) faithful exercise of Christian discipline?

_____ 3. Which of the following two are recognized by Reformed/ Presbyterian churches as sacraments: (a) profession of faith; (b) baptism; (c) marriage; (d) footwashing; (e) Lord's Supper; (f) ordination?

_____ 4. Which of the following describe church discipline: (a) members who care about each other; (b) good education programs and teaching; (c) helping members who wander from the church; (d) all of these; (e) all but "b"?

_____ 5. Good preaching should first of all be (a) Christ-centered; (b) entertaining; (c) person-centered; (d) dramatic and emotional; (e) good storytelling.

_____ 6. The line "I believe in the holy catholic church" comes from (a) Pastor Lew; (b) the Belgic Confession; (c) the Bible; (d) the Apostles' Creed.

_____ 7. Oneness, holiness, and catholicity are known as (a) marks of the true church; (b) attributes of the church; (c) the mission statement of the church; (d) the vision statement of the church.

_____ 8. Incarnation refers to (a) Jesus' intense suffering; (b) Jesus' exaltation; (c) Mary's sinlessness; (d) the Son of God taking on human flesh; (e) an ordinary man becoming like God.

_____ 9. Which best describes the relationship between Christ's human nature and his divine nature: (a) divine dominates the human; (b) are indistinguishable in one person; (c) distinct but connected; (d) totally separate?

_____ 10. Christ suffered and died to make amends for our sins. We call this (a) the atonement; (b) the virgin birth; (c) the incarnation; (d) the transfiguration; (e) sanctification.

BIBLE TRIVIA

1.   5.

2.   6.

3.   7.

4.   8.

VIDEO DISCUSSION GUIDE

1. Define the following terms related to the church:

- Church invisible:

- Church visible:

- Church militant:

- Church triumphant:

- Church as organism:

- Church as institute:

2. What are the four "P"s that describe the main values of the church?
   - P-1:

   - P-2:

   - P-3:

   - P-4:

3. Which of the four "P"s do you personally think is most important? Which ones does your congregation emphasize? Which ones would you like to see your congregation emphasize more?

4. Read Ephesians 4:1-6. What do you think this passage has to say to your church? Try making up a slogan or blurb that's based on this Bible passage and that's aimed at your congregation.

5. When have you really felt the oneness with other Christians that Ephesians 4:1-6 talks about?

6. Pastor Lew comments on the importance of members using their gifts to serve their Lord and their church. Think about the abilities, gifts, interests, and character traits that God has given you. Then jot down one way you could use (or are using) one or more of your gifts to serve God and your congregation.

7. Remembering our congregation in our prayers is one way we can all serve. List some areas of challenge or concern to pray about.

SACRAMENTS: BAPTISM

REVIEW QUIZ
(fill in blank)

1. All true believers of all times and places are known as the church
   _____.

2. The church in heaven is known as the church _____
   _____.

3. The church as official organization is called the church as
   _____.

4. The church fighting Satan and evil is the church _____
   _____.

5-6. Two of the four "P"s that describe the task of the church are
   _____ and
   _____.

7-8. Two of the marks of the true church are _____
   _____ and _____.

9. Christ's paying the price of our sin by his suffering and dying is called
   _____.

10. The name Jesus means _____.

BIBLE TRIVIA

1.   5.

2.   6.

3.   7.

4.   8.

VIDEO DISCUSSION GUIDE

1. What does the water in baptism represent? (See Acts 22:16 and Romans 6:1-4.)

2. What is the covenant of grace, and what is its connection to baptism, especially infant baptism? (See Genesis 17:7, 11-12; Galatians 3:29.)

3. How does Pastor's Lew's "rich uncle" story help us understand why we baptize infants, even though they don't have a clue about what's going on?

4. Christians in the Baptist tradition do not believe in infant baptism. They believe in the immersion of adult believers. Why? (See Romans 6:4; Matthew 3:13-17; Acts 16:31-34.)

5. What did you learn from the baptism scene on the video?

6. If you were baptized as an infant, how has God worked, and how is God presently working in your life to lead you to claim the promises God made in baptism? If you have not yet been baptized, how is God presently working in your life for your salvation?

SACRAMENTS: THE LORD'S SUPPER

REVIEW QUIZ

(true|false)

T | F

☐ | ☐ 1. The water in baptism represents the nourishment we receive from Christ.

☐ | ☐ 2. Baptism can be viewed as being buried with Christ and rising to new life.

☐ | ☐ 3. There are many texts in the Bible that directly command us to baptize infants.

☐ | ☐ 4. The key reason for baptizing infants is that they are included in the covenant.

☐ | ☐ 5. Reformed/Presbyterian churches only baptize infants, never older children or youth or adults.

☐ | ☐ 6. Calvinists believe that immersion is wrong.

☐ | ☐ 7. Pastor Lew's "rich uncle" story helps us understand why we baptize infants, even though they don't have a clue about what baptism means.

☐ | ☐ 8. Proper administration of the sacraments is one mark of the true church.

☐ | ☐ 9. The four "P"s of the church are proper worship, preservation of tradition, propagation, and people's needs.

☐ | ☐ 10. Christ dying for our sins in our place is called the incarnation.

BIBLE TRIVIA

1.   5.

2.   6.

3.   7.

4.   8.

VIDEO DISCUSSION GUIDE

1. Definitions

- closed communion:

- close communion:

- open communion:

- R:

- R:

- R:

- F:

- F:

- two hands:

- sacraments:

2. Article 33 of the Belgic Confession says that sacraments are "visible signs and seals of something internal and invisible." A sign is a picture, something we can see that gives us a message of some kind; a seal is a kind of guarantee, an assurance that something is true and will work. So how is the Lord's Supper a sign and a seal?

3. Would it be all right to substitute potato chips and Coke for the bread and wine or grape juice of the Lord's Supper? Why or why not?

4. What is the covenant of grace? With whom was it made? What did God promise to do? What is our response supposed to be? What does the covenant of grace have to do with the Lord's Supper?

5. Why do you think God gives us the sacraments?

6. Talk about your own experiences in taking communion (or in anticipating taking it if you don't currently participate in the sacrament). What benefits do you receive or expect to receive? Does the way the sacrament is presented in your congregation help or hinder you?

DISPENSATIONALISM

REVIEW QUIZ

(true|false)

T | F

☐ | ☐   1.   The two sacraments in the Reformed tradition are the Lord's Supper and baptism.

☐ | ☐   2.   Sacraments are called signs because they point out or give us pictures of what Jesus did for our salvation.

☐ | ☐   3.   Sacraments are called seals because they guarantee that God's promises of salvation are real.

☐ | ☐   4.   The bread and the wine in the Lord's Supper point us to the way God cares for us by supplying our daily food.

☐ | ☐   5.   The bread and the wine are symbols that in themselves contain nothing of the meaning of what they represent.

☐ | ☐   6.   The "three 'R's" of the Lord's Supper are remember, repent, and rededicate.

☐ | ☐   7.   The "two 'F's" of the Lord's Supper are fellowship and fearing God.

☐ | ☐   8.   The "two hands" of the Lord's Supper are God's hands reaching down and the elder's hands passing us the sacraments.

☐ | ☐   9.   The covenant of grace was originally made between God and Abraham and his descendants.

☐ | ☐   10. The covenant of grace extends to all believers today.

BIBLE TRIVIA

1.   5.

2.   6.

3.   7.

4.   8.

VIDEO DISCUSSION GUIDE

1. Dispensationalist churches believe history is divided into
   _____ distinct time periods or dispensations.
   During each time period God _____ the way in
   which he deals with his people; he also tests obedience in different ways.
   There is little or no continuity between time periods.

   - First dispensation: innocence

     _____ and _____
     lived in a state of perfection or innocence. God said,
     "_____ me and live forever." But they
     disobeyed and death entered the world.

   - Second dispensation: conscience

     Sin awakened human conscience. God said, "Follow your moral sense
     and obey me." A man named _____ and his
     family did exactly that. But the rest of the world did not. As a result,
     God was forced to _____.

   - Third dispensation: human government

     During this time God related to people through authority figures
     and leaders. But, as indicated by the _____ of
     _____ , the leaders disobeyed. And so God gave up his
     plan of world government and confused and scattered the people.

- Fourth dispensation: patriarchs (or promise)

  God called _____ and gave him many
  great promises. He began a great new nation of God's people
  called _____. Under the leadership of
  _____, God's people were led out of slavery.
  But even great leaders weren't enough to convince them to obey God.

- Fifth dispensation: law

  At Mount _____, God began a new era of
  relating to his people Israel through external laws and procedures.
  But once again God's people didn't listen. They failed to keep
  God's law, and so they ended up in _____ in
  Babylon, though a remnant returned to Jerusalem. At the end of this
  dispensation, God sent _____ to fulfill the law, but
  the people rejected him and killed him.

- Sixth dispensation: grace and the church

  At _____ the Spirit descended and the
  Christian _____ began. God relates to
  his people through their acceptance or rejection of Jesus Christ.
  This is the dispensation in which we are living; it will end when
  _____ _____.

- Seventh dispensation: kingdom or millennium

  The final dispensation will be Christ's _____-year
  reign in Jerusalem on the throne of David. During this time of
  prosperity and peace, _____ will be given
  another chance to accept Christ. When this dispensation ends,
  _____ begins.

2. How does the view of Calvinist Christians generally differ from the
   view of dispensational Christians? For the Calvinist, what holds history
   together?

3. How does the view of dispensational Christians differ from that of Calvinist Christians on the following issues?

- the Bible

- God

- the church

- infant baptism

4. "How can you be optimistic about the future when you look at the past and present? It's pretty obvious, isn't it, that Satan's in control of this world? Any thinking person can see that the world isn't getting any better. War, poverty, racism, violence, starvation, AIDS, greed, shootings at schools . . . you name it, we've got it. So you're a Christian—what difference does that make, other than giving you a way out of this mess after you die?"

How would you respond if someone said this to you?

5. A long time ago, a Reformed statement of faith was written that began with the question "What is your only comfort in life and in death?" A different way of asking that question is, "What is your only hope for the future?" Please think about that, and, if you're willing, share your response with the group.

END TIMES: PREMILLENNIALISM

REVIEW QUIZ

(fill in the blanks)

1. Some Christian churches believe that history is divided into _____ _____ dispensations.

2. These churches teach that today we are living in the dispensation of _____.

3. This dispensation began with Pentecost and extends until _____ _____.

4. The previous dispensation, which began with Moses and ended with the death of Christ, is that of _____.

5. Dispensationalists reject infant baptism because they do not believe it replaces _____, which they say took place in a different dispensation and has nothing to do with us today.

6. Calvinists believe that history is not divided into various dispensations or periods of time; instead it is _____ _____.

7. Calvinists say that God's basic way of dealing with his people does not _____.

8. The Lord's Supper includes _____, repentance, and rededication.

9. The covenant of grace was originally made between God and Abraham, but now extends to _____.

10. Sacraments are both signs (pictures) and _____ (guarantees) of Christ's atoning work for us.

BIBLE TRIVIA

1.   5.

2.   6.

3.   7.

4.   8.

VIDEO DISCUSSION GUIDE

1. What support does Revelation 20:1-3 give for the millennium or dispensation of one thousand years? What do premillennialists believe?

2. Fill in details of each of the following events that many dispensationalists and all premillennialists believe will happen during the final dispensation (the millennium or thousand years). The passages listed are those often given in support of this view.

   • The trumpet and the rapture (1 Thessalonians 4:13-18)

   • The tribulation and the mark of the beast (Matthew 24:4-8, 22; Revelation 13:16-18)

- The millennium

    a. Jesus' public return with believers (Matthew 24:30-31)

    b. Satan locked in the pit (Revelation 20:1-3)

    c. Christ's glorious reign of a thousand years begins
       (Revelation 20:1-4)

- Satan briefly unleashed, destroyed by Christ (Revelation 20:7-10)

- Final judgment (Revelation 20:11-13)

3. Many Christians today—including many of those who teach "believer's baptism by immersion"—hold to some version of the above "end time events." What is your personal reaction to the premillennialist view? What seems reasonable to you? What do you wonder about?

4. Next week's session will look in detail at the Calvinist view of the end times (especially Revelation 20). For now, just indicate very briefly what Calvinists think will happen at the end of time.

5. Suppose you knew that Jesus would return in exactly one year. How might you change your life?

END TIMES: THE REFORMED VIEW

REVIEW QUIZ

1-8. Put the following "end time" events in the order in which premillennialists believe they will happen (1 by the first event, 2 by the second, and so on):

____ final judgment

____ sound of trumpet

____ Satan briefly unleashed but defeated

____ the seven years of tribulation and the mark of the beast

____ the rapture of all believers to be with Christ in the air

____ the thousand-year reign of Christ (millennium) from Jerusalem

____ Jesus' public return with believers begins the millennium

____ Satan locked in the pit

9-10. true/false statements:

T | F

☐ | ☐   9. Dispensationalists say we are living in the dispensation or time block of law.

☐ | ☐   10. Premillennialists believe that Christ's return will precede and bring about his thousand-year reign of peace and prosperity.

BIBLE TRIVIA

1.   5.

2.   6.

3.   7.

4.   8.

VIDEO DISCUSSION GUIDE

1. Get the picture of the Reformed view of the end times by filling in the missing words in each event described below:

   - A loud _____, the voice of an _____, and a _____ call of God will announce the return of Christ (1 Thessalonians 4:16). _____ on earth will see him coming!

   - The _____ will be raised first. Then those who are still _____ on the earth will be instantly changed to immortal beings and will meet _____ in the air (1 Thessalonians 4:16-17).

   - Then God will _____ this old world (2 Peter 3:10).

   - The earth will then be _____ (2 Peter 3:13; Revelation 21:1).

   - Christ will _____ the living and the dead (Revelation 20:12). Those who have rejected Jesus will ____ _____ (v. 15), but those who love Jesus will live with him forever in the beautiful _____ (21:1-3).

2. How does the Reformed view of the end times differ from the premilliennialist view?

3. Suppose that we die before Jesus comes. What happens next?

4. When you think about the final judgment, which all Christians agree is coming, what are your feelings? Do you tend to see it as a time of celebration, as Pastor Lew suggests, or as a scary time of having to give a public accounting of all your sins?

5. How do Calvinists generally interpret the thousand years, the binding of Satan, and the other events mentioned in Revelation 20:10?

6. Read Revelation 21:1-5, 22-27. What do you think living in the new heaven and new earth will be like? What will not be present there? What will be present?

BEING DISTINCTIVELY REFORMED

REVIEW QUIZ

(true|false)

T | F

☐ | ☐   1. The Bible clearly predicts seven years of tribulation.

☐ | ☐   2. Premillennialists believe that believers will escape the tribulation by being raptured into the air to meet with Jesus.

☐ | ☐   3. We (Calvinists) believe in the literal (actual) thousand-year reign of Christ (the millennium).

☐ | ☐   4. We believe that Jesus will come just once to judge the living and the dead.

☐ | ☐   5. We believe that when we die, our souls or spirits go immediately to be with Jesus.

☐ | ☐   6. When Jesus returns, our bodies will be resurrected and reunited with our souls.

☐ | ☐   7. After the judgment we will live with God and Jesus in the air.

☐ | ☐   8. The covenant of grace was originally made between God and Moses.

☐ | ☐   9. We and all believers in Jesus are included in the covenant of grace.

☐ | ☐   10. Christ's atonement for our sins makes us "at one" with God.

BIBLE TRIVIA

1.   5.

2.   6.

3.   7.

4.   8.

VIDEO DISCUSSION GUIDE

1. What's the first and most important thing you should say to someone who asks you what it means to be Reformed or Calvinistic? (See John 3:16; Ephesians 2:8.)

2. As Calvinists, we interpret Christianity as the Reformers did, especially John Calvin. So we ought to know something about the man whose ideas helped shape our faith tradition. Identify the following:

   • when Calvin lived

   • the city Calvin reformed

   • the famous book Calvin wrote

   • how Calvin's influence spread

   • churches today that are "Calvinistic"

3. Like all true churches, Reformed churches place a high value on Scripture (see 2 Timothy 3:16). What evidence do you see in your congregation and around you that the Bible is crucial to our faith and our daily living?

4. Calvinism is marked by holding to certain creeds and confessions that summarize biblical teachings from the Reformed perspective. Identify your church's creeds and confessions. Why are they necessary?

5. One idea that distinguishes Calvinists from, say, Lutherans or Baptists or Methodists, is our emphasis on the sovereignty of God. When you think of the awesome power and supremacy of God, what comes to mind? How should God's sovereignty make us feel? (See Psalm 8:1; Psalm 24:1.)

6. Calvinism stresses God's decrees, including election and predestination. What do these terms mean and how does believing them help us? (See Ephesians 1:4-5.)

7. Calvinists believe in living disciplined Christian lives with definite standards and rules (see James 1:27). Give some examples of this from your own life. How can this kind of disciplined living help Christians?

8. Calvinists are a "reforming" people—that is, we test our ideas and practices (see Romans 12:2) against what the Bible teaches. Give an example that shows how your congregation or denomination is reforming. What is being evaluated or changed or initiated?

9. Calvinists believe in a unified or covenantal view of history (see Genesis 17:7). What does this mean?

10. Most Calvinists have what's called a "world-and-life-view." We'll look at this more closely next week. For a clue about what it means, look up 1 Corinthians 10:31.

LIVING AS A CHRISTIAN

REVIEW QUIZ

(fill in the blanks)

1. The most important answer to the question "What does it mean to be Reformed?" is _____

    _____.

2. Churches in the Reformed tradition were much influenced by the ideas of _____, a writer and theologian who worked to reform the city of _____.

3. As Calvinists we rely heavily on _____ as the foundation of our faith and the guide to living.

4. Calvinist churches use certain _____ as summaries of biblical teachings.

5. Calvinists emphasize God's control over all things. This is called the _____ of God.

6. Reformed people believe the Bible teaches election. Election refers to _____

    _____.

7. Calvinists believe in living _____ Christian lives with definite standards and rules.

8. Being Reformed means that we are willing to test our ideas and practices against the Bible and _____ them if necessary.

9. Calvinists have what's often called a "world-and-life-view." This means that all aspects of life are dedicated to God's

   _____.

10. Premillennialists claim that when Jesus returns after the tribulation, he will initiate a _____-year reign of peace and prosperity from the city of Jerusalem.

BIBLE TRIVIA

1.   5.

2.   6.

3.   7.

4.   8.

VIDEO DISCUSSION GUIDE

How do we live as Christians in today's world? Imagine that you have a tough decision to make. As a senior in high school, you have to decide what college to attend. Your choices boil down to just two: a local Christian college or a university several hundred miles away from home. Let's further assume that the two choices are equally appealing. While there are obvious differences in size and location and attractions, both offer a good education and housing at about the same cost. What's more, you'll have friends at both institutions. So how do you decide?

Talk about how each of the six approaches outlined in today's video would help you (or not help you) decide what to do. Also talk about how each approach sees the relationship between the Christian and world. What are the strengths and weaknesses of each approach?

1. What would Jesus do?

2. Bible verse approach

3. Opposition mode

4. Common sense method

5. Love is the answer

6. Understanding and transforming the world (world-and-life-view)

PROFESSION OF FAITH/ RECOMMITMENT

REVIEW QUIZ

(true|false)

T | F

☐ | ☐ 1. One approach to determining how to live as a Christian in this world is to ask what Jesus would do in this or that situation.

☐ | ☐ 2. If we look hard enough, we can find a specific verse in the Bible that tells us what to do in a given situation.

☐ | ☐ 3. According to the "opposition mode," Christians should become involved in the world only when necessary and then in moderation.

☐ | ☐ 4. In the "common sense" method, the sacred and the secular exist side by side but are separate from each other.

☐ | ☐ 5. In the "love is the answer" approach, the most important consideration in any situation is loving yourself and thinking of your own well-being.

☐ | ☐ 6. The Calvinist view of the relationship between the world and Christians is called a "world-and-life-view."

☐ | ☐ 7. Calvinists believe that it's the job of Christians to understand and, when necessary, transform the world.

☐ | ☐ 8. Jesus is both real God and real man.

☐ | ☐   9. Profession of faith is one of three sacraments recognized by most churches in the Reformed tradition.

☐ | ☐   10. Churches in the Reformed tradition emphasize the sovereignty of the saints.

BIBLE TRIVIA

1.   5.

2.   6.

3.   7.

4.   8.

VIDEO DISCUSSION GUIDE

1. How do Calvinists view the world? What is our task in it?

2. Pastor Lew gives some examples of ways that Christians are working to change some aspects of our society for the better. Give some additional examples that you've heard about or participated in. How have you or other Christians from your church or youth group or school attempted to "transform" some part of our society or world that needs healing?

3. What reason for professing our faith does Romans 10:9 give?

4. Pastor Lew implies that if we wait until we're "ready" to profess our faith, we'll never do so. Do you agree? Why or why not? What helped some of the teens on the video know that they were ready to take a stand for Jesus?

5. Which is more offensive to you: people who have publicly professed their faith but who don't live as Christians or people who believe in Jesus but who won't publicly confess his name? Why?

6. Which, if any, teaching(s) of the church do you feel uneasy or unclear about? Should these feelings keep you from professing your faith? Why or why not?

7. Did any of the comments from the teens on the video help you in some way? Offend you? Raise a question for you? Express your own feelings? Please explain.

8. This is the last question in this course—and the most important. Where are you today in your own walk with Jesus? Share as little or as much as you wish. If you've professed your faith, you may want to say what it means to you today. If you've not done that, you may want to talk about your reasons for waiting. The important thing is to express your feelings honestly and sincerely.